PROTECT YOURSELF ONLINE

ONLINE SCAMS

by J. K. O'Sullivan

BrightPoint Press

San Diego, CA

© 2022 BrightPoint Press
an imprint of ReferencePoint Press, Inc.
Printed in the United States

For more information, contact:
BrightPoint Press
PO Box 27779
San Diego, CA 92198
www.BrightPointPress.com

ALL RIGHTS RESERVED.

No part of this work covered by the copyright hereon may be reproduced or used in any form or by any means—graphic, electronic, or mechanical, including photocopying, recording, taping, web distribution, or information storage retrieval systems—without the written permission of the publisher.

LIBRARY OF CONGRESS CATALOGING-IN-PUBLICATION DATA

Names: O'Sullivan, J. K., author.
Title: Online scams / by J. K. O'Sullivan.
Description: San Diego, CA : BrightPoint Press, [2022] | Series: Protect yourself online | Includes bibliographical references and index. | Audience: Grades 7-9
Identifiers: LCCN 2021036474 (print) | LCCN 2021036475 (eBook) | ISBN 9781678202484 (hardcover) | ISBN 9781678202491 (eBook)
Subjects: LCSH: Internet fraud--Prevention--Juvenile literature. | Computer crimes--Prevention--Juvenile literature. | Internet--Security measures--Juvenile literature.
Classification: LCC HV6773.15.C56 O88 2022 (print) | LCC HV6773.15.C56 (eBook) | DDC 364.16/3--dc23
LC record available at https://lccn.loc.gov/2021036474
LC eBook record available at https://lccn.loc.gov/2021036475

CONTENTS

AT A GLANCE	**4**
INTRODUCTION A TEXT FROM A STRANGER	**6**
CHAPTER ONE WHAT ARE ONLINE SCAMS?	**12**
CHAPTER TWO THE HISTORY OF ONLINE SCAMS	**28**
CHAPTER THREE RECOGNIZING AN ONLINE SCAM	**40**
CHAPTER FOUR AVOIDING ONLINE SCAMS	**58**
Glossary	**74**
Source Notes	**75**
For Further Research	**76**
Index	**78**
Image Credits	**79**
About the Author	**80**

AT A GLANCE

- Scammers target people online. They steal from or cheat others for personal gain.

- There are different types of online scam techniques.

- Phishing is one trick scammers use. It is a way to get people to turn over personal information.

- Fraud has always existed. Lottery and vacation scams are some examples of fraud.

- The internet gave scammers new ways to cheat people. As the internet grew, online scams grew too.

- Scammers change their tactics often. It is important to be up-to-date on new types of scams.

- There are ways to tell a real request for information from a fake one. It is possible to identify online scams.

- Everyone should protect their personal information online. Creating strong passwords is one way to do this.

- Government agencies track online scams. They enforce the law. Anyone can report scams to these agencies.

- Staying safe online is a challenge. Protecting private information takes effort.

INTRODUCTION

A TEXT FROM A STRANGER

Noah was eating lunch at school. His phone buzzed. A text notification flashed on the screen. "This is your UPS driver. We are trying to deliver your package. We cannot reach you. Please click this link to reschedule."

Noah's mom had ordered a pair of earbuds for him. She used her credit card

Unexpected texts can be confusing—and they might be sent by a scammer.

for the order. It was strange that he would get a message. But he really wanted the earbuds. He had been waiting a long time. He clicked the link. The link led to a screen.

Online passwords must be changed right away after an online scam happens.

The UPS logo was on top. "Reschedule delivery," the screen read. There was an empty text box. A note indicated he should enter his name and email address there. They already had that information, Noah thought. Why did they need it again? Noah entered the information anyway. He went to class.

At home, he told his mom about the text. "Show it to me," she said. When he did, she shook her head. "It is a **phishing** scam," she said. "You didn't click it, did you?" Noah's heart sank. He nodded. "We need to change your passwords," she said. Noah opened up his phone settings. He got to work on making his phone safe from scammers.

ONLINE SCAMS 101

Phishing is a type of online scam. This type of fraud targets people through websites, emails, and texts. Scammers use different ways to steal information and money from others.

Other online scams include shopping scams and bank fraud. Scammers try to win the trust of their targets. Then they take advantage of them. Scammers might also trick victims into downloading software. That software can reveal private information. Scammers use this information to access accounts.

Online scams can be prevented by understanding how they work.

It is possible to avoid online scams. People can do this by being alert and educated. These scams are always changing. But there are ways for people to stay safe.

CHAPTER ONE

WHAT ARE ONLINE SCAMS?

Fraud is a crime done for financial or personal gain. Online scams are a type of fraud. Online scammers lie and trick people. Scammers try many ways to get money from victims.

Scammers target victims on computers and phones. They send emails and texts to kids, teens, and adults. They trick victims

People can lose money after they are tricked into giving out their personal banking information.

into sending money. They may ask for credit card numbers or bank account information.

A scammer might ask for personal information. Scammers know that accounts are protected by passwords. But personal information protects accounts too.

A scammer might ask for the name of a favorite pet. They might ask for the city you were born in. They might ask for a street address. Sometimes they ask for a **Social Security number**. This type of information is used to reset forgotten passwords. With these details, a scammer hopes to access a victim's bank account.

TYPES OF SCAMS

Scammers use many different methods to cheat people. One of the most common scams is called phishing. Scammers phish by sending an email that appears to be from a real company. The email will contain

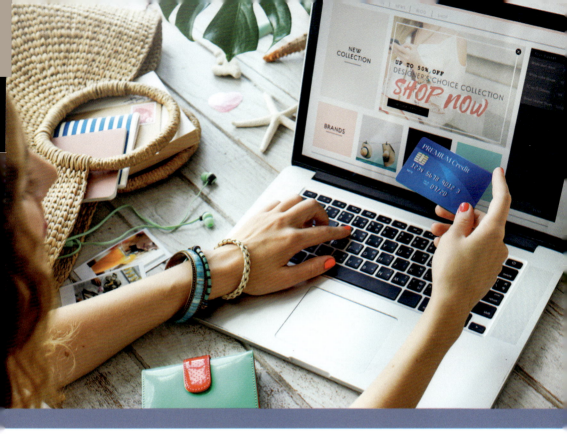

Online shopping is fast and convenient. But people should be aware of online scams.

a request. The request tricks the receiver into clicking a link. The link might lead to a website that looks like a real company website. The target of the scam might trust the site. The target types in a password. The scammer steals the password.

Then the scammer uses this password to try to access the victim's online accounts.

Scammers create fake shopping websites. The site asks for bank information to complete a purchase. But the purchased item is never sent. The scammer keeps the funds. A different type of scam involves offering discount luxury items. The item that is sent is a cheap **knock-off**. There are also package delivery scams, like the one that happened to Noah.

Scammers may claim to be from a company tech support department. They earn the trust of the victim. They ask for remote access to the victim's computer.

They say they need to make a repair.

The scammers get remote access. They

can now install software. They can steal

passwords and financial information. "They

offer you a security package and if you are

convinced that your system is infected,

then you have to pay hundreds of dollars

WHO DO SCAMMERS TARGET?

Scammers target children, teens, and adults. They may target kids on popular gaming platforms. They know families sometimes share a computer. They might use a child's log-in to access parents' financial information. Older people who may not be very good with technology are also targets of online scammers.

to remove **malware** from your system,"
says tech support scam expert Najmeh
Miramirkhani.[1]

HOW SCAMMERS APPEAL TO EMOTIONS

Some victims fall for online scams by
accident. Other times scammers play on
victims' emotions. Then they can take
advantage of their victims.

Some online scammers try to
scare victims. A scammer might say
that there is an urgent problem. The
scammer might send a fake bill that
must be paid. A scammer might make
threats. Scammers might say they have

Scammers may make threats or demand that fake bills be paid.

embarrassing information. They will release it unless demands are met.

Scammers play on a victim's hopes and dreams. Scammers might say a victim has won a contest. To claim the prize, the person must click a web link. The victim must supply some personal information. Scammers often target students. A common scam claims the student has won a scholarship. To receive it, the student must provide a bank account number.

Scammers might appeal to a person's desire for fame. Scammers may offer a modeling contract. They might offer a chance to be in a film. They might offer to publish a person's writing or artwork. The scammer says the person must supply some money up front. When the money is sent, the promised results are never delivered.

Online scammers may appeal to teens by promising a modeling or film contract.

Some scammers appeal to a victim's sympathy. The scammer might claim a family member needs medical help and can't afford it. The scammer collects online donations for the treatment. But the stories are fake. There is no medical problem. The scammer keeps the money for personal use. This type of scam is sometimes used after a disaster happens. People donate money to help those affected. But the money just goes to the scammer.

One type of scam starts with a romantic text or email. Scammers pretend to be interested in the victim. Then they ask for money. These scammers also look for victims who are gamers. They might invite a player on a game platform to click a link.

Gamers are often the target of online scammers.

They might say they know someone who has a crush on them.

Scammers also target job seekers. A person may be offered a position. To be paid, the victim must supply a bank account number. Another scam involves a fake investment opportunity. The scammer asks the victim to invest money in a company. The victim sends the money to the scammer's bank account. The scammer disappears.

HOW SCAMMERS USE TECHNOLOGY

Scammers do not always ask for financial information directly. They may find a way to get access to private files. They can do this by tricking people into downloading malware. Malware is short for malicious software. A person might download it accidentally by clicking on a link. The malware will be hidden on the victim's computer. Malware may track what a user does online. When the victim logs into a bank account, the scammer can get access to it.

SCAMMERS PLAY GAMES ONLINE

Kids, teens, and adults love online games. Scammers know this. One popular scam is to pretend to help players in these games. The scammers might offer a code to help a player reach a higher level. They might help them win in-game items. The player supplies credit card information to get the code. The scammer steals the credit card number. The victim might not realize the information has been stolen. Scammers might spend a lot of money before the victim knows what has happened.

One type of malware is called ransomware. This is a kind of malware that can lock a person's files. When the files are locked, the victim cannot access them. The scammers will demand money to unlock them. This scam is also used against companies and even governments.

Scammers sometimes target a major company's website. They break through the company's security. This is called hacking. Hackers can sometimes carry out scams. They steal passwords from a company's website. This is called a password breach. Scammers use stolen passwords to try

Malware can lock computer files.

to access users' accounts. "Hackers and cybercriminals are largely driven by financial gain," says Patrick Wardle, a **cybersecurity** expert.[2] They try to steal financial information this way. Password breaches have become a common problem online.

CHAPTER TWO

THE HISTORY OF ONLINE SCAMS

Fraud has existed for a long time. Before the internet, there was mail fraud. There was petty theft. The internet gave scammers new ways to trick people. As the internet grew, online scams grew too. Now, about one in ten adults falls victim to internet fraud each year. As many as 1.3 million children have their identities

Adults, teens, and children can all fall victim to online identity theft.

stolen online each year. It is more common now to be the victim of online identity theft than to fall victim to a pickpocket on the street.

WELL-KNOWN SCAMS

One of the best-known online scams is called the Nigerian prince scam. In this scam, the victim receives an email asking for money. This money is said to be for an investment. The author of the email clams to be a prince or government official. The scammer says there will be a big payoff for the victim. The scammer asks for a bank account number and other information.

In 2018, the Nigerian prince scam got more than $700,000 from people who fell for it.

The email claims the investment will be returned. Scammers sometimes claim they are in trouble. They say they need financial help.

This scam was very successful in the early years of the internet. The scam appeals to victims' sympathy. Some believe they will make money. Many people sent money to the scammers. They never heard from them again. Many people have learned about the Nigerian prince scam and don't fall for it. But some haven't heard of it. They still fall for this scam. If only a few people fall for it, the scammer still makes money.

Another famous scam tells victims they inherited money from an unknown relative. This scam is written by someone claiming to be the relative's lawyer. The inheritance may be millions of dollars. The lawyer asks for a bank account number. The letter says this is needed to deposit the inheritance.

The lawyer may ask the person to wire money to a bank account. The victim sends the money. The scammer is never heard from again.

The lottery scam is another kind of scam. In this scam, a victim is told he or she has won a lottery. To receive the winnings, the

THE NIGERIAN PRINCE SCAM IS NO JOKE

The Nigerian prince scam is so common that it has appeared in shows such as *The Office*. It has been mentioned in jokes on *Saturday Night Live*. There is even a movie called *The Nigerian Prince*. It is about an American teen who gets involved in his cousin's scams. These jokes and references have led to unfair negative stereotypes about Nigerians. Nigeria is located in West Africa. It is the world's seventh-most populous country.

Many people fall victim to online lottery scams.

victim must supply a bank account number.

"These things are incredibly common, and the chances of somebody running across them are very high," says scam investigator Steven Baker. "Unfortunately, a lot of people lose a lot of money to them."[3]

ALWAYS INNOVATING

Many people know about common internet scams. But there are always new ones. Scammers follow trends. They change their approach based on what is happening in the world. Around holidays, they use new shopping scams. They responded to the COVID-19 pandemic too. They took advantage of people's health concerns.

When a new technology is created, scammers figure out how they can use it

Holiday shopping scams change each season.

to cheat people. "Scammers are constantly seeking opportunities to find vulnerable victims," says Anja Solum, a project manager at ADT Security.[4]

PRIVATE AND GOVERNMENT CYBERSECURITY

Online attacks increase each year. That increases the need for better online security. Cybersecurity is now a big business. It protects consumers, companies, and governments. Many companies specialize in cybersecurity. Some companies have cybersecurity experts on staff.

Government agencies also protect against online fraud. The Federal Trade Commission (FTC) began protecting consumers online in 1994. But scams kept popping up. By 1999, the number of

Companies hire cybersecurity experts to protect their online businesses.

internet fraud crimes had greatly increased.

Now there are more federal and local

agencies monitoring online fraud.

Scammers quickly adapt to find new ways to cheat people. But security companies and governments are finding new ways to track and stop them. Individuals can also help to stop scammers. Learning about online scams is one way to do that.

A FUTURE IN FIGHTING CYBERCRIME

Scamming is just one kind of internet security problem. Scammers and hackers also try to steal secrets from governments and companies. New software and hardware can protect these files. Cybersecurity is one of the fastest-growing jobs fields today. There will be even more demand for these experts in the future.

CHAPTER THREE

RECOGNIZING AN ONLINE SCAM

Online scammers often trick victims by posing as real businesses. They may pretend to be friends or family members. They carry out scams through fake websites. They also send emails filled with lies. But there are ways to tell a real email or website from a fake one.

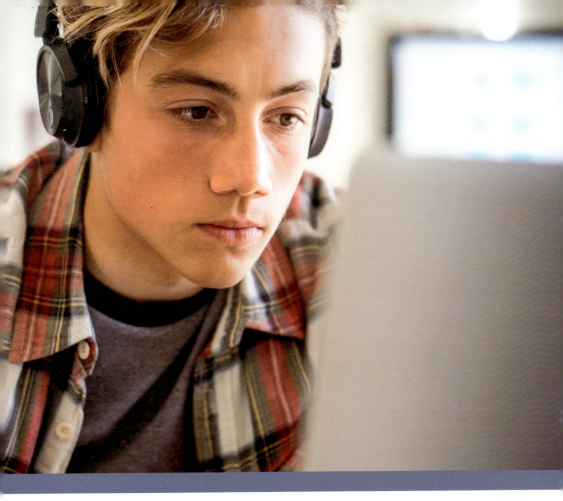

It is easy to be tricked by an online scam email.

Email scams are very common. "They're the easiest to pull off, and don't require any real programming skills on the part of the bad actor," says Chris Hauk, a consumer privacy expert.[5]

IDENTIFYING AN ONLINE SCAM

There are ways to identify email scams. Some of the clues are easy to spot. For instance, words may be misspelled. However, sometimes victims will not read the emails closely and might miss the typos. Scammers often try to make their emails look official. They copy the language of a real prize or scholarship offer. They may even use the words *official notice* in the email. This is not something a real company usually does. But many people are fooled. They may answer and send the scammer money. Email scammers often try to

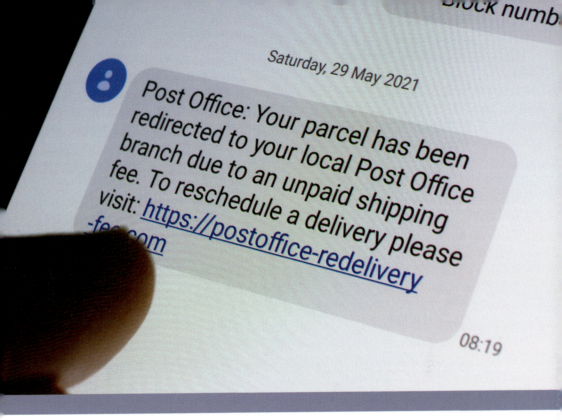

Online scammers often use text messages to get the attention of potential victims.

pressure victims into responding. They use words like *urgent* or *respond immediately*.

Some scammers use a different approach. They are friendly and informal. They might start their emails with "My Dear" or "Dear Friend." They want it to seem like their victim already knows them. Sometimes a scammer pretends to be a friend or relative. They do this through email or social media. Scammers might take photos from Facebook or Instagram. Then they use the photos to make a new profile. This profile is a fake one. They try to connect with the person's friends this way. Then they ask the friends for personal information.

An offer or request that requires a bank account number is suspicious. It should be treated with caution. An honest company gives customers several ways to pay.

Scammers tell customers they must pay a certain way.

FAKE WEBSITES

Scammers make false websites that look like real ones. A real website includes information so visitors can contact the site owner. But a fake website usually

SPOTTING A FAKE WEBSITE

Check the address bar to see if a website is real. Web browsers show an alert on suspicious websites. This alert will say "not secure." A fake website might use a web address similar to a real address. But it might use a slightly different spelling. Or it may include an extra word. Users should pay careful attention to the web address.

Fake websites often try to get victims to download documents.

doesn't have this. Fake websites often include poor spelling or grammar. Many pop-up windows might mean a website is fake. A fake website might urge visitors to download documents. Real websites have security certificates. Fake websites don't, but they might have something that looks like one. Scammers hope victims won't look too closely.

Scam websites have features that make a victim believe the site is real. There might be a phone number or address on the site. The scammer believes the victim won't use this information.

ONLINE SHOPPING SCAMS

Fake shopping websites are common. They might show luxury items at a big discount. They claim to be selling famous brands. These websites often feature clothes

Fake shopping websites offer the latest fashions at prices that are too good to be true.

and handbags. These appeal to teens looking for the latest fashions. Shoppers purchase the item but get a knock-off item or nothing at all.

Experts say users should pass up offers that look too good to be true. "At the end of the day, that's what they are," says cybersecurity expert Yair Levy.[6]

FAKE CHARITIES

Scammers often pretend to be a charity. They look for donations after natural disasters such as floods or wildfires. They say the money will go to people needing help. Instead, the scammer keeps the money. Other times scammers say they are raising money to help sick children. They try to play on victims' emotions. They take advantage of victims' kindness and generosity. Often victims are made to feel selfish if they do not donate. These scammers also have a second victim, as the money does not reach the people that need help.

Like other online scammers, they may use a website that looks real. It may have a name similar to a well-known charity. The name may be spelled a bit differently. They may set up fake Facebook accounts.

With a little bit of research, people can avoid getting scammed by fake charities.

They tell a tragic story and ask for donations. The payments are made through a website or PayPal. The receipt may not have the charity's name on it. Or there may not be a receipt at all. Donors should look up charities online to see if they are real. It is best to donate directly to real organizations instead of giving to email or social media requests.

CROWDFUNDING SCAMS

Many new businesses raise funds online. They use a site like Kickstarter to raise money. This platform allows many people to donate. People enjoy helping a small business. They are also promised a reward when the business reaches its goal. Scammers can also be found on

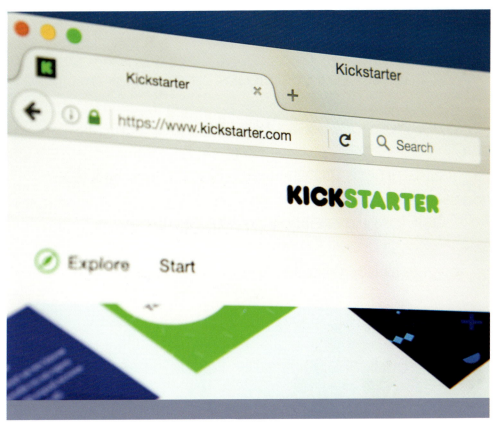

Kickstarter can help people turn their dreams of launching a business or creative project into a reality.

this site. But there are ways to identify

them. Each campaign includes a profile of

its creator. A scammer may not have much

information there. They may not list other

projects. Honest businesses will often have

a track record of success. They will also
answer questions online and give updates.
Scammers will go silent. Scammers will also
ask for unrealistic amounts of money.

Another popular site is GoFundMe.
This is used by people who need money
for medical bills or other needs. These
campaigns often go viral. Many people have
been helped by strangers. But scammers
use this site too. Some scammers fake
illness. Or they set up a fund for someone
else and keep the money for themselves.
Donors may never get their money back.
It can be hard to spot a scam online. The

campaign should state how the money will be used. Beware of campaigns that do not show a clear plan. However, scammers sometimes share a fake plan. Donors can Google the name of the organizer and "scam" or "complaint." This will show if they have been involved in scams before.

A FUN QUIZ WITH NOT-SO-FUN RESULTS

It can be fun to take online quizzes. They promise to reveal something about personality traits. But hackers use these quizzes to steal personal information. A quiz might ask for information that is used in security questions. Some quizzes require the quiz-taker to click on a link. That link might lead to a dangerous download. Avoid taking a quiz that asks for personal information or an email address.

To avoid scammers, it's smart to do a little research before donating to a GoFundMe campaign.

Avoid requests that offer little information. Also, check the social media accounts of the person requesting money. Scammers will often create a fake profile just before starting a GoFundMe campaign. If there is little activity shown online, it might be a scammer. It is always a good idea to ask the organizer direct questions. Scammers may not respond. Or they might provide information that does not make sense.

CHAPTER FOUR

AVOIDING ONLINE SCAMS

Experts say that each new email or website might be dangerous. Each new site must be treated with suspicion. Something that looks like it comes from a friend might not be. It might be from a scammer who has hacked the friend's account. It's important to be aware of these dangers online.

Sometimes a scam email can look like it's from a friend.

New scams are launched all the time. Websites such as Fraud.org monitor new scams. Government agencies such as the FTC post this information too. These reports help the public recognize scams. Those who know about scams can avoid them.

PASSWORD PROTECTION

Password protection is important. All passwords should be changed regularly. The same password should not be used for multiple accounts. Many sites require security questions and answers. Those answers should be easy to remember but difficult for a scammer to guess.

Some websites offer **two-step verification** as a security measure. This system requires two methods to prove ownership of an account. The user might have to enter a password. Then she has to use her phone to confirm she wants to

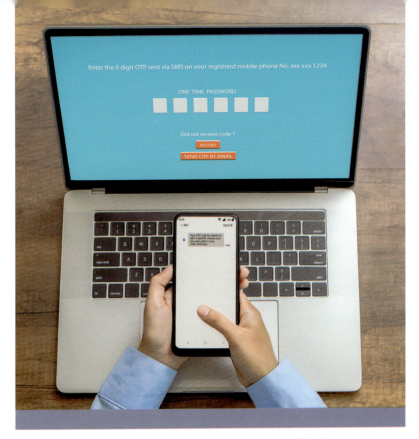

Two-step verification is a proven way to keep online accounts secure.

log in. Two-step verification keeps people's accounts more secure. It's unlikely a scammer will have both the password and the phone to get into a person's account.

Protecting passwords is important. But it's not the only way to stay safe from online scammers. Private information such as

Social Security numbers, home addresses,

and family information should not be shared

with unfamiliar people online. Scammers

can use this information to open their own

accounts in the victim's name.

WHAT IS A STRONG PASSWORD?

Many sites suggest using a strong password. The site might suggest a password created by a computer. This is usually a very long password. It is made up of letters, numbers, and special characters. Site users can use this password or make one up. Passwords should not be obvious. An obvious password would be a phone number or birth date. A good password should not include a common sequence of numbers, such as 01234.

PUBLIC WI-FI

It's easy to access Wi-Fi in public places. Many people like to hang out in cafés and libraries and use the internet. They log on to social media or do work. Libraries have public computers that are free to use. But online scammers target Wi-Fi connections in public places. It is safer to use a Wi-Fi network that requires a password. These are called **secure networks**. Each user's information is protected.

Users need to be careful when using public Wi-Fi. They should stay away from banking websites. Others using the Wi-Fi

People should be cautious when using public Wi-Fi so scammers don't steal passwords or personal information.

can easily steal their banking information. Users must log out of personal accounts on a public computer. Passwords can be used to access users' data.

UP-TO-DATE HARDWARE AND SOFTWARE

The **operating system** (OS) is a computer's basic software. Keeping the OS updated protects against malware. The OS provides built-in protection. Computer companies continue to find ways to fight new types of malware.

Software can protect against malware. This is called antivirus software. It tracks

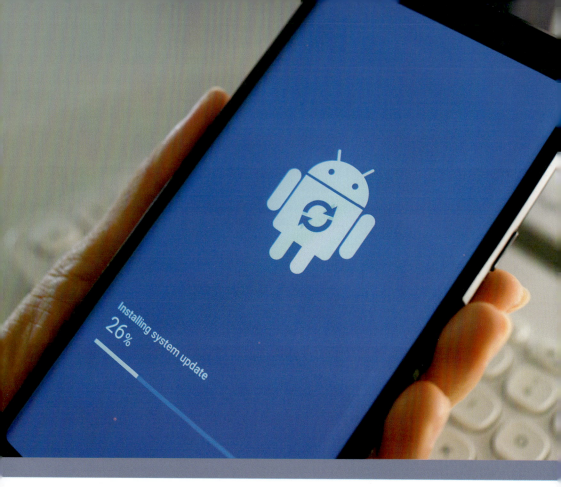

Keeping a device's operating system updated helps protect against malware.

information from the computer to the internet. If there is suspicious activity, an alert lets the user know. When a website is unsafe, a warning will alert the user not to click on the site. If a user downloads a dangerous file, the software will isolate the file. Then it cannot damage the computer.

CELL PHONE AND SHOPPING SCAMS

Sometimes scammers use cell phone numbers to target victims. They use these

WHAT IS ENCRYPTION?

Online scamming and hacking is like eavesdropping. Eavesdropping is when someone listens to another person's private conversation in a public place. The internet is a very public place. Hackers and scammers use technology to eavesdrop online. Encryption is a way to scramble information. That way, hackers and scammers can't understand it. Most email service providers use encryption. Up-to-date hardware and software includes encryption too.

calls to run scams. The best way to avoid them is not to answer calls from unknown numbers. "Criminals can push out billions of automated calls," says Aaron Foss. "But they need a human being to answer."[7] Foss is the founder of Nomorobo. This company blocks unwanted scam calls.

It is possible to block phone calls from unfamiliar numbers. Some phone companies do this. They can identify potential scam calls too. It is also possible to block emails or texts from unfamiliar addresses. This makes it harder for scammers to succeed.

Blocking calls from unfamiliar numbers is a good way to avoid scammers.

To avoid falling for a shopping scam, compare prices for similar items on different sites. It might be exciting to find a bargain. But if a price looks too good to be true, it probably is. The item that is advertised might be a fake. Or the item may not even

be delivered.

REPORTING SCAMS

There are government agencies that

can help victims of scams. They collect

reports about scams from people. They

assist companies in tracking data about

their online sales. This helps to identify

and stop scammers. There are consumer

protection agencies at the local, state,

and federal levels. Nonprofit groups also

protect consumers from online scams.

They provide information to help people.

They show victims how to take action if

Reporting scams to consumer protection agencies can help others avoid them.

they have been scammed. "If you see something out there that looks fraudulent, report it," says cybersecurity expert Arun Vishwanath.[8] Reporting scams can help others avoid them.

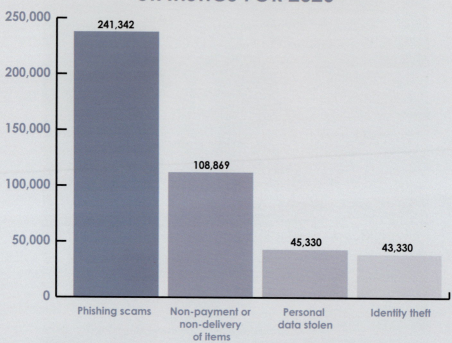

Source: Federal Bureau of Investigation, "2020 Internet Crime Report," *Internet Crime Complaint Center*, March 17, 2021. www.ic3.gov.

More people fall victim to phishing scams than any other type of online scams.

Parents and teachers can be good resources. They can help kids and teens avoid online scams. If the scam has happened, they can prevent further damage. It can be scary to be the victim of an online scam. Being honest and sharing information with a trusted adult is the best response. It makes it possible to undo the damage. And it helps the victim be safer in the future.

Online scammers always try to find new tactics. It is easy to fall victim to scams. But there are many groups that aim to protect consumers. Learning about online scams is the first step toward internet safety.

GLOSSARY

cybersecurity
protection for online networks and information; also called internet security

knock-off
a poorly made item designed to look like a high-quality product

malware
dangerous software that harvests information or harms a victim's computer

operating system
the basic software that runs a computer

phishing
an online scam that steals information through fake emails and websites

secure networks
computer networks that are safe from hackers

Social Security number
a unique number each US citizen receives that is used for official federal government business

two-step verification
a method of online security that requires two different ways to confirm identity

SOURCE NOTES

CHAPTER ONE: WHAT ARE ONLINE SCAMS?

1. Quoted in Steven Melendez, "The Awful, Fast-Growing Tech Scams Fleecing the Elderly Out of Millions," *Fast Company*, May 10, 2019. www.fastcompany.com.

2. Quoted in Stuart Dredge, "Here's What Cyber Security Experts Teach Their Kids About the Internet," *Business Insider*, August 11, 2014. www.businessinsider.com.

CHAPTER TWO: THE HISTORY OF ONLINE SCAMS

3. Quoted in Mallika Mitra, "Here's How Lottery Scammers Are Conning Americans," *Money*, February 18, 2021. www.money.com.

4. Quoted in Megan Leonhardt, "'Nigerian Prince' Email Scams Still Rake in Over $700,000 a Year—Here's How to Protect Yourself," *CNBC*, April 18, 2019. www.cnbc.com.

CHAPTER THREE: RECOGNIZING AN ONLINE SCAM

5. Quoted in Laurie Budgar, "How to Spot Apple ID Phishing Scams," *Reader's Digest*, June 15, 2021. www.rd.com.

6. Quoted in Kaya Yurieff, "Watch Out for These Holiday Shopping Scams," *CNN*, December 3, 2018. www.cnn.com.

CHAPTER FOUR: AVOIDING ONLINE SCAMS

7. Quoted in Laura Daily, "Phone and Email Scammers Have Pivoted During the Pandemic. Here's How to Protect Yourself," *Washington Post*, November 4, 2020. www.washingtonpost.com.

8. Quoted in Jeddy Johnson, "How to Protect Yourself from Online Shopping Scams," *WKBW*, November 27, 2020. www.wkbw.com.

FOR FURTHER RESEARCH

BOOKS

Carrie Anton, *Smart Girl's Guide: Digital World: How to Connect, Share, Play, and Keep Yourself Safe*. Middleton, WI: American Girl Publishing, 2017.

A. R. Carser, *Protect Your Data and Identity Online*. San Diego, CA: BrightPoint Press, 2022.

Ashley Nicole, *Privacy and Social Media*. Broomall, PA: Mason Crest Publishing, 2019.

INTERNET SOURCES

"Eight Common Scams Targeted at Teens," *Investopia*, November 30, 2020. www.investopedia.com.

"How to Avoid the Worst Online Scams," *Wired*, March 22, 2020. www.wired.com.

"How to Recognize and Avoid Phishing Scams," *Federal Trade Commission*, n.d. www.consumer.ftc.gov.

WEBSITES

Frauds and Scams
www.consumerfinance.gov/consumer-tools/fraud/

This US government website offers advice on how to avoid online scams.

Report Scams and Fraud
www.usa.gov/scams-and-frauds

This website provides links for reporting scams at both the local and national levels.

Scams and Safety: Internet Fraud
www.fbi.gov/scams-and-safety/common-scams-and-crimes/internet-fraud

The Federal Bureau of Investigation outlines the most common types of internet fraud and links to examples.

INDEX

bank account, 13–14, 20, 23–25, 30, 32–34, 44
bank information, 16

charities, 49–50, 52
COVID-19 pandemic, 35
credit card, 6, 13, 25
cybercrime, 39
cybercriminals, 26
cybersecurity, 27, 37, 39, 49, 71

encryption, 67

Facebook, 44, 50
fake websites, 40, 45–47
Federal Trade Commission (FTC), 37, 59
financial information, 17, 24, 27
fraud, 4, 10, 12, 28, 37–38

GoFundMe, 54, 57
government agencies, 5, 37, 59, 70

hackers, 26, 39, 55, 67

identity theft, 30, 72
Instagram, 44
internet, 4, 28, 31, 35, 38–39, 63, 66–67, 72–73

Kickstarter, 52
knock-off, 16, 49

malware, 18, 24–25, 65

Nigerian prince scam, 30, 32–33

operating system (OS), 65

password breaches, 26–27
passwords, 5, 9, 13–15, 17, 26–27, 60–63, 65
personal information, 4–5, 13, 20, 44, 55
phishing, 4, 9–10, 14, 72

ransomware, 26
remote access, 17

secure networks, 63
security certificates, 47
Social Security number, 14, 62
software, 10, 17, 24, 39, 65, 67

technology, 17, 24, 36, 67
two-step verification, 60–61

web browsers, 45
Wi-Fi, 63

IMAGE CREDITS

Cover: © Syda Productions/Shutterstock Images
5: © fizkes/Shutterstock Images
7: © DGLimages/iStockphoto
8: © fizkes/Shutterstock Images
11: © fizkes/Shutterstock Images
13: © Antonio Guillem/Shutterstock Images
15: © Rawpixel.com/Shutterstock Images
19: © Andrey Popov/Shutterstock Images
21: © Marcos Homem/iStockphoto
23: © Prostock Studio/Shutterstock Images
27: © rawf8/Shutterstock Images
29: © Pond Saksit/Shutterstock Images
31: © Michael Burrell/iStockphoto
34: © Antonio Guillem/iStockphoto
36: © Cleardesign1/iStockphoto
38: © Gorodenkoff/Shutterstock Images
41: © Perfect Wave/Shutterstock Images
43: © mundissima/Shutterstock Images
46: © Anfisa Che/Shutterstock Images
48: © martin-dm/iStockphoto
51: © monkeybusinessimages/iStockphoto
53: © Chris Dorney/Shutterstock Images
56: © Flamingo Images/iStockphoto
59: © Marian Fil/Shutterstock Images
61: © KT Stock photos/Shutterstock Images
64: © Blue Titan/Shutterstock Images
66: © TY Lim/Shutterstock Images
69: © fizkes/Shutterstock Images
71: © BravissimoS/Shutterstock Images
72: © Red Line Editorial

ABOUT THE AUTHOR

J. K. O'Sullivan is an author and educator who has written more than 20 books for young people.